Part I
Faith and Politics

KILLING THE MYTH OF SEPARATION OF CHURCH AND STATE

A Christian Worldview Perspective

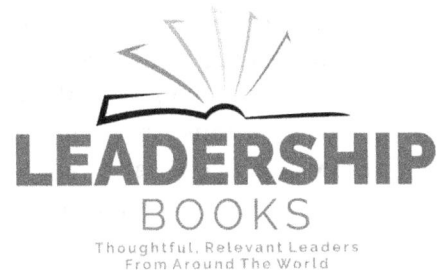

FREDDY DAVIS

Killing the Myth of Separation of Church and State: A Christian Worldview Perspective

2nd Edition Copyright © 2024 Freddy Davis

Formerly published as Separation of Church and State: A Christian Worldview Perspective © 2022

All Rights Reserved

Published by Leadership Books, Inc. Las Vegas, NV – _New York, NY

LeadershipBooks.com

ISBN:

978-1-951648-72-5 (Hardcover)

978-1-951648-73-2 (Paperback)

978-1-951648-79-4 (eBook)

All Rights Reserved. No part of this publication may be reproduced, distributed, or transmitted in any form or by any means, including photocopying, recording, or other electronic or mechanical methods, without the prior written permission of the publisher, except in the case of brief quotations embodied in critical reviews and certain other noncommercial uses permit-ted by copyright law.

Contents

Introduction 1

Part I Faith and Politics 3

   Chapter 1 5

     Separation of Church and State vs. Separation of Faith and State

   Chapter 2 17

     Worldview Beliefs in the Political Arena

   Chapter 3 31

     Worldview Foundations in Political Systems

Part II Politics and Values 43

   Chapter 4 45

     A Christian Worldview Perspective on Freedom

   Chapter 5 51

     Human Rights, Constitutional Rights, and Christian Rights

   Chapter 6 57

     Are Christian Values Necessary for Freedom in America?

   Chapter 7 67

     Can America Be Moral Without God?

Chapter 8 75
What Do 21st Century American Values Look Like?

Part III Faith and Actions 83

Chapter 9 85
Citizenship Stewardship

Chapter 10 95
Should Christians Be Politically Active?

Concluding Observations 109

Introduction

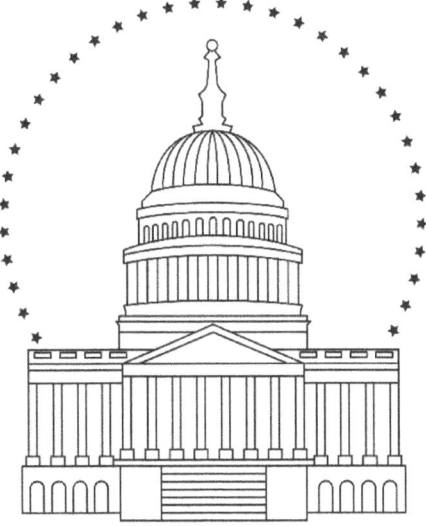

It may interest you that I originally wrote this book for a special purpose, and it was not published for general consumption. For several years, I worked in a Christian ministry to the state legislators in the State of Florida. In that ministry I would often meet with the various legislators and their staff, pray for them, and provide Christian devotional material for them. Every year, at the beginning of each legislative session, I made it a point to give each of them some kind of special gift that would be relevant to their work, but also be a witness for Christ. In 2016, I wrote this book, had it published, and gave it to them.

Introduction

Now, though, I believe it is time to share it with the general public. I believe all Christian citizens need to get up to speed on this issue.

As a writer on the topic of worldview, I deal with a lot of different themes. It is, first of all, my intention to help people understand the idea of worldview in general. It is only when we grasp the full scope of possibilities that any particular expression of life can be fully understood.

Additionally, as a Christian, I believe that the biblical worldview represents the way reality is actually structured. So, another focus of my writing is to help people understand the "biblical worldview." With that, it becomes possible to take virtually any subject, discover the biblical worldview perspective of that subject, then compare it to how other worldview beliefs treat it. We can do this with virtually any subject i.e., theology, philosophy, psychology, sociology, biology, business, education, and so on.

This brings me to the more focused purpose of this book. Over time, as I have written about worldview beliefs, the issue of politics has always been a hot topic of interest. In this book, you will find a compilation of ten articles that have been adapted and combined to share a Christian worldview perspective on politics and political activity. It is my hope and desire that you will find in these pages not only some new perspectives about politics, but, as God leads, it will also provide motivation for you to become more actively aware and engaged in the critical issues and far-reaching effects that the political process plays in our lives and in the lives of our fellow citizens.

Chapter 1

Separation of Church and State
vs.
Separation of Faith and State

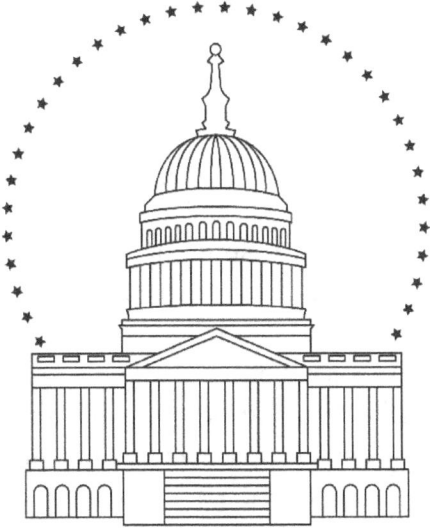

We hear all the time that there must be separation of church and state. There is a particularly big hue and cry from people who want to eliminate all vestiges of religion from the public square. This is the point of view of those we often refer to as secularists.

They believe that their "secular" approach, which leaves mention of God out of everything public, is the only way to accomplish what the Constitution says. They want government to be run without any faith or religious influence whatsoever. For the most part, these are people who are very well intentioned, but do not grasp a very important principle about the nature of faith. They believe that the values of the Christian faith can somehow be separated from other values that are neutral.

The truth is, though, there is no such thing as "neutral" values. All values come from some philosophical system. While the "secularists" try to assert that their approach is totally faith neutral, their belief is, in fact, as much a faith position as is any other religious belief.

What they are really advocating is a "separation of faith and state" using beliefs that are themselves an expression of a faith system. As such, the attempt to separate "religious" values from the operation of government is impossible. What is actually being advocated is not the removal of religion from the public square, but the exchange of one set of religious values for another. The attempt to create this shift is, typically, based on two basic arguments that are used as pretexts to promote the belief that "separation" means eliminating religious values from the public square.

The first pretext is promotion of the concept of "separation of church and state." The other is to assert that the establishment clause of the first amendment to the U.S. Constitution prohibits any expression of Christian ideas in the public square. Let's take a few moments to explore how this actually plays out. With this, we should be able to make some distinctions that help us get down to the actual truth of the matter.

The True Meaning of "Separation of Church and State"

Contrary to the assertion of those who are trying to push Christian beliefs out of the public square, the concept of "separation of church and state" is not in the Constitution. In fact, it is not a part of U.S. jurisprudence at all. The term itself was the offshoot of a phrase Thomas Jefferson used in a letter he wrote in 1801 to the Danbury Baptist Association in Danbury, Connecticut.

Jefferson was, in this letter, responding to a communication from the Association expressing concern that religious freedom was not adequately protected in their state constitution. In this conversation, there was never even a thought that the influence of Christian beliefs should be somehow expunged from the public square – in political discourse or anywhere else.

The reason for the concern of the Danbury Baptists was that it was not uncommon during that period of history for there to be an official state sponsored church. This was the tradition that existed at that time in Europe, and many of the settlers who came from Europe were satisfied to bring that tradition to a new American government. The Connecticut Baptists did not want the government to have any influence over the free exercise of religion, so they petitioned Jefferson to make sure freedom of religion was

Chapter 1

protected. As we know, this protection was inserted into the U.S. Constitution in the 1st Amendment.

What modern secularists have tried to do is take the concept and make it mean something different from what was originally intended. The law concerning religious freedom was designed to keep government from prescribing religious practice for the citizenry, not to keep citizens from expressing their faith in the public square.

The ideas that led to the effort to reverse the American approach originated in Europe. This concept emerged initially in France and Spain, as their Constitutions favored a "secularist" approach that viewed the concept of "separation" as being a way to keep religious notions from influencing the operation of the state. As such, secular (primarily atheistic) beliefs became dominant. This point of view was picked up by American secularists who have been working continuously to insert this interpretation into American law.

The bottom line is, however, that the concept of "separation of church and state" does not mean what modern secularists claim – and it has no place in American law. In fact, what they deem it to mean is a literal impossibility. In their effort to try and scrub religious values from American society, they are not working to keep the state from establishing a state church – which is what the first amendment is actually about. That is not even in the conversation.

What they are actually trying to do is prevent Christian *value*s from having any place in the development and implementation of laws. In its place, they want to substitute a different set of values. This is a very different thing than what the 1st Amendment even addressed.

The Concept of "Separation of Faith and State"

What the secularists are really proposing is not the separation of church and state, but the separation of faith and state – to a degree. Actually, the only faith they want to separate from the state is the Christian faith. As it turns out, it is the values of the Christian faith that formed the basis for American society at its founding. Such concepts as the rule of law, freedom of conscience, the value of life, free enterprise, ethical behavior based on objective criteria, and private ownership of property are all values that emerged from the teachings of the Christian faith. When secularists put forth their version of separation, what they really mean is they want to replace those Christian values with relativism in law, political correctness, a low value of life, economic redistribution, ethics based on relativistic values, and public ownership of property. What is not said is that this point of view is just as much based on a faith foundation as the one they are trying to replace.

The truth is, the values of the secularists are not "non-religious." They emerge directly out of a naturalistic worldview – which is a faith position. It is the belief that all of reality can be accounted for based on the natural laws of the universe. However, there is no empirical basis for values based on this belief. As such, it represents a religious point of view.

If you were to speak to secularists to point out that their approach is based on religious beliefs, most of them would be totally flabbergasted. They honestly believe that setting aside "God/religion" from the public square is a completely religiously neutral position. The truth, though, is entirely different. Their "secularism" is a religious point of view.

In order for something to be neutral in the way they conceive it, a point of view cannot have a faith foundation. It must be based strictly on objective, experimentally verifiable facts. The problem is, this secularist point of view is not based on facts. It is belief system based on a set of philosophical presuppositions.

Let's look for a moment at this secularist philosophy. In order for that point of view to be true, there are several things that must not only true, but verifiable using experimental science.

> ***1. Everything that makes up the material universe must have a natural origin.*** The problem is, there is no science able to demonstrate that to be true. It is simply assumed to be true because a supernatural reality is dismissed out of hand based on naturalistic philosophical beliefs.
>
> ***2. Life must have a natural origin.*** Again, there is no science to demonstrate this is even possible. It is

assumed by Naturalists to be true, not because of science, but because the possibility of the existence of God is dismissed out of hand based on their philosophical beliefs.

3. The variety of life forms that exist on earth must be accounted for using natural means. Once again, there is no experimental science able to show this to be true. In spite of the various theories and speculations that have been put forth, scientists do not know of any natural biological process that allows individual life forms to evolve beyond certain limits. The belief in naturalistic evolution is purely based on philosophical presuppositions, not on science.

4. Consciousness must have a natural origin. The same problem exists here as with all the others. The speculation as to the origin of consciousness is based on naturalistic philosophical presuppositions, not on science.

As can be seen, the "secular" position is not based on observable facts. It is an expression of faith. It is, essentially, a religious point of view. As such, the attempt to purge expressions of the Christian faith from the public square is not an attempt to get religion out of public life. Rather, it is an attempt to replace one faith foundation with an entirely different one. So the question then becomes, "Why should the values of a 'secular' religion replace the values of a theistic one?"

Chapter 1

At this point, we must say that no one is talking about creating a theocracy. I don't know of anyone who wants to take a sectarian set of rules and make them the law of the land. That would, by default, create a state church – the very thing the founders were determined to prevent. The real issue at hand revolves around which set of values will hold prominence in the public square.

By their unthoughtful assertions, many people seem to believe that it is possible for there to be a values free public sector. But that is simply not true. There will be some set of values that dominate society. And whatever that set of values turns out to be, they will be based on a faith foundation.

Individuals don't check their personal beliefs and morality at the door when they enter public service. They bring them in and act in their public life based on those beliefs. If they believe in a high value of life, they work to promote that point of view. If they believe in a low value of life, they work to promote that. If they believe in free enterprise, they actively advance policies that promote free enterprise. If they believe in economic redistribution, they work toward that goal. And the list could go on.

The point is, no matter what "beliefs" people bring to the table, they work to promote those "beliefs." In other words, they live out their faith life in their public service. It is impossible for human beings to do otherwise.

So How Should Citizens Respond to This?

So the bottom line is, "separation of church and state," as promoted by secularists, is a bogus argument. No one is proposing that the government establish a state church. Additionally, the argument that promoting Christian values (not sectarian rules) in the public square is wrong because it entangles church and state is also bogus. Promoting Christian values in the public square is no more a violation of the "separation of church and state" than promoting secular values.

Since some set of values will dominate culture, the real question at hand is, "Which values should that be?" Should it be values that promote life, liberty, and the pursuit of happiness, or values that promote death, bondage and public ownership of property?

In the end, the citizenry must make that decision. But the decision should not be made based on the use of oppressive laws to push one set of values out of the public square. It should be made in an environment where the majority is able to truly express its will.

So, how should citizens respond to this situation? Let's look at several suggestions.

1. Understand the Playing Field

First, we cannot push back against that which we do not understand. The first thing people must do is to make an effort to truly understand the faith nature of secularism and how it leads to beliefs that are contrary to America's founding principles. Efforts must then be made to expose the deception. A secular approach to operating government is simply not value neutral. It expresses a particular value system that is based on a faith foundation. With this understanding, it becomes possible to expose the deceptive efforts of those who say they are trying to keep "religion" out of the public square.

2. Remember we are Stewards of God

In American culture, the rulers of the land are the citizens. The representatives we elect and those who work in other areas of government are not our rulers. Rather, they are our proxies. As individual Christians, we are responsible before God to accept our stewardship responsibility in the political arena. And that stewardship responsibility is to manage those who represent us. We are responsible before God to do what we can to promote His will and His ways in our culture. An important part of that is to influence the political system.

3. Act as Faithful Stewards

The work of a steward involves acting. Different people are called by God to do it in different ways, but everyone has some responsibility in that arena. We must discern God's leading about how to act, then do the work. First and foremost, every citizen should vote. In the system of government God has placed us in, that is the very least we can do.

But there are many other possibilities, as well. Some will be led to make this a full-time enterprise by, for instance, running for office, promoting policy in some particular area, working in the government bureaucracy, or promoting the election of particular candidates. Others may feel led to do some of these things part time or to act completely as civilians. This work can be done by petitioning one's representatives, diligently praying for elected officials, or directly engaging them with the gospel. Every believer needs to discern God's leading and act.

Contrary to the beliefs of many, separation of church and state is not a legitimate point of view when it is used to advocate for the expulsion of Christian values from public life. In fact, it is totally illegitimate, and all citizens should push back against that thinking.

Chapter 2

Worldview Beliefs in the Political Arena

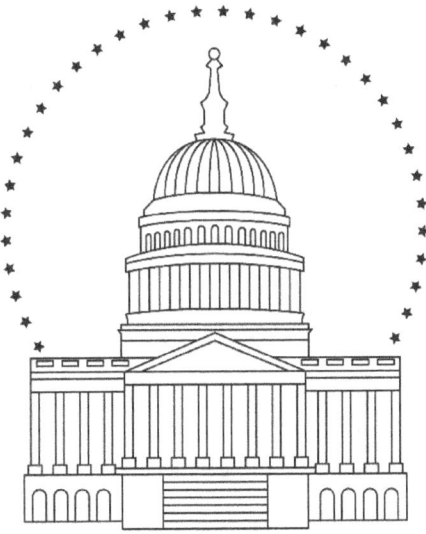

Most people don't realize the extent to which a person's worldview beliefs affect the different parts of their lives. The tendency is to relegate this topic to the "religious" arena. But the truth is, it impacts EVERY area of life. It speaks to science, morality, law, politics, economics, and, literally, every other area of life you can think of.

Chapter 2

When we consider American politics, there are, actually, a number of different points of view that get expressed in the public square. That being said, there are two that are head and shoulders above all the others – liberalism and conservatism. And, you guessed it, these two perspectives are based on opposing worldview foundations that can easily be identified and analyzed.

What is Liberal and Conservative?

But before we get into the details of these two viewpoints, we need to say something about the words themselves. Liberalism and conservatism, in the broadest sense, do not have a point of view all their own. Something is always liberal or conservative in relation to something else. What may be liberal in one context may be conservative in another. As such, we have to identify the context before this makes complete sense.

Conservatism is a point of view that, basically, wants to preserve (conserve) the status quo. So, once we identify the initial foundation, conservatives are those who want to maintain it.

Liberalism, on the other hand, is a point of view that wants to change (liberate) the status quo. Again, once we identify the initial foundation, liberals will be the ones who want to change it.

What is Liberal and Conservative in America?

America was founded by people who believed in God, and who established the institutions of the society on principles from Christian Theism. This includes such concepts as an absolutely authoritative foundational document, the rule of law, equal justice under the law, separation of powers, due process, equal opportunity for all, ownership of private property, individual responsibility, freedom of conscience, and the like. Conservatives, then are those who believe in these founding principles and work to see that they continue.

Liberals, then, would be those who seek to change that. In modern American society, liberalism is built, specifically, on a naturalistic worldview foundation. The basic principles that emerge out of this is relativism and collectivism. It is understood from this naturalistic viewpoint that, since there is no such thing as the supernatural, human beings are the ones who must establish the principles of society – there is no other possibility. And the principles used to accomplish this are based on naturalistic presuppositions. Survival of the society and personal satisfaction are the bottom line.

While the terms liberalism and conservatism tend to mostly have political connotations, the truth is, the beliefs that inform these two positions play out in virtually every area of life. Let's take a brief look at some of the more prominent ones.

Chapter 2

Theology

Conservative

Conservative theology is most closely associated with Theism – belief in God. This was the default position of the founders, and informs the approach they used for establishing the various cultural institutions of American society. Conservative beliefs are most closely associated with the Christian faith (or what is often referred to as the Judeo-Christian ethic), and takes its guiding principles from the teachings of the Bible. It is based on the belief that God is the Creator and Sustainer of the material universe and that man is a fallen creature.

Liberal

Liberal theology is most closely associated with Naturalism. In its most natural form, liberal theology follows naturalistic belief – that is, it does not acknowledge the existence of any kind of supernatural reality. It's theology is expressed as some form of Atheism – the assertion that God does not exist.

That being said, there are those who self-identify as liberals who are adamant that they do believe in God, and many are even active in churches that have traditionally been associated with the Christian faith. What we generally find in these situations, however, is a Christian form that overlays a naturalistic core. This kind of theology uses religious, even Christian, vocabulary, but basically redefines the words in ways that express naturalistic concepts. The most prominent forms of "Christian" theology in this category include liberation theology, neo-orthodoxy, existential theology, and postmodern theology. The doctrines associated with these forms typically do not believe God to be a personal being who can be known in a personal relationship, nor does it acknowledge the Bible to be a sure revelation from God.

Philosophy

Conservative

Conservative philosophy, in America, is based on the tenets of Christian Theism. This involves a type of dualism where both body and mind are acknowledged. As such, it is possible to combine both faith and reason into the consideration of the basic topics of philosophy – reality, knowledge and values.

Liberal

Liberal philosophy is based on the tenets of Naturalism. As such, it is expressed as a type of monism where all of reality exists within the confines of the physical universe (i.e., all of reality is material). The operation of the mind is understood to be built upon the belief that what we perceive as "mind" is actually nothing more than the natural operation of the physical brain. An understanding of the basic topics of philosophy (reality, knowledge and values), then, must be based only on what exists in the material world.

Biology

Conservative

The conservative approach to understanding biology is based on a theistic belief about the structure of reality. Using this worldview approach, the most fundamental concept of biological understanding rests upon the belief that the origin of life, and the existence of the variety of life forms on earth, is all accounted for by the supernatural creative activity of God. Conservative biology sees no problem in believing both that God created life AND that the material manifestations of life can be studied by science.

Liberal

Liberal biology is founded upon Naturalism, and is based on the belief that natural biological evolution alone accounts for the existence of life and for the variety of life forms that exist on earth. Naturalism assumes that there is no such thing as a supernatural reality, so the only means by which life could possibly have come into existence and emerged into current forms is by natural means. All of life is understood to be purely an expression of the material universe.

Psychology

Conservative

For conservatives, psychology relates to both an objectively real spiritual element as well as a physiological one. Human beings are acknowledged to be spiritual as well as physical creatures. That being the case, conservative psychology is based on concepts that are best explained based on a dualism of mind and body. It operates off of the belief that God has made human beings to be self-conscious spiritual beings housed in a physical body.

The soul relates specifically to the spiritual side of an individual. It is that part of a human being which is not physical. So, when individuals have issues that trouble the soul, it relates specifically to a person's sin against God, not merely to things that cause internal conflict. That being the case, the solution to these soul issues requires making things right with Him. At the same time, the soul exists on earth in a physical body and cannot be separated from it. It must be understood and expressed through a physical body. As such, the soul is expressed and can be partially understood physiologically, as well.

Liberal

Psychology in liberalism is based on the naturalistic belief that human beings are purely physical animals with no spiritual part. This leads to methods of dealing with the human mind and human behavior which are purely physiological. Using the common naturalistic approaches to psychology, curing human psychological problems is a matter of fixing wrong thinking by using behavioral techniques and chemical substances. The soul, in liberal psychology, is nothing more than an expression of the physical self.

Sociology

Conservative

While conservative sociology is interested, to a degree, in all of the institutions found in society, there are three that are especially emphasized because they are seen to be the most foundational based on a biblical perspective. The three are: traditional family, church, and state.

Conservative sociology begins with the theistic assumption that God created the world and gave instructions regarding the proper order of human groupings based on His purposes. It is understood that there is a way society ought to be ordered, and it is up to the members of society to try and order it that way.

Liberal

Liberal sociology is founded upon the naturalistic worldview assumption that there is no such thing as a supernatural reality. As such, humans do not exist for any transcendent purpose, but are merely animal creatures that have evolved from mindless matter. It is believed that this evolutionary process developed in a way that caused human beings to be social animals as a means of survival. Since it is believed that there exists no transcendent purpose for mankind, there is also, by extension, no purpose for society – other than survival. Additionally, without a transcendent being to provide direction, there is also no prescription as to how society ought to be ordered. It can become whatever the people in the society decide is appropriate.

Ethics and Morality

Conservative

Conservative ethics, established on a Theistic worldview foundation, is based on the concept of moral absolutes. Theism asserts the existence of a transcendent God who has revealed to mankind what is right and wrong. God is understood to have a particular way that He wants human beings to act, and has revealed that desire to humanity. In the case of Western conservatism, that relates specifically to the values revealed in the Bible.

Liberal

Liberal ethics emerges out of Naturalism and is based upon the concept of moral relativism. Liberals acknowledge no form of transcendent existence. As such, there is no one outside of the material universe capable of creating or sharing moral information. Thus, all morality and ethics must be created by human beings – either by using societal consensus or the imposition of the moral preferences of those in power. Since no absolutes are acknowledged, the standards of morality may change as the societal situation or the individuals in power change.

Law

Conservative

Conservative law begins with the assumption that God exists and has revealed His will concerning what is right and wrong. The belief is that human law, then, should reflect these instructions from God – at least on the basis of principle, if not in the specific laws themselves.

It is the contention of conservative law that God has established material reality based on His conception of order. His system is based on an absolute standard that does not change. This order is, first of all, reflected in the laws of nature. Secondly, it is reflected in the revealed laws that God has given to mankind through His revelation. This revealed law casts light on the true nature of humanity and on God's purpose for the advancement of society.

Liberal

Liberal law is based on a naturalistic worldview foundation and is expressed in the principle of positive law. Law from a naturalistic worldview perspective has no objective or transcendent basis. Rather, it is based on the perceived needs of society and/or the personal inclinations of those in power. There is no other possibility. And, since there is no objective foundation for law, the laws themselves, and even the foundational principles for interpreting law, can be changed at any time based on contemporary circumstances.

Politics

Conservative

The topic of politics is important for conservatives because government is one of the institutions that are understood to have been established by God in order to facilitate the accomplishment of His purposes for mankind. Conservative politics is specifically based on theistic concepts which recognize that God has revealed moral principles by which man should govern society. Since the work of government is understood to have been ordained by God, human beings are charged with understanding His purpose, and carrying out the work of government based on that purpose. God has revealed two primary roles that a government is supposed to play – to protect the innocent and punish the guilty. In doing this, order and justice are maintained in society. It is the duty of politicians to manage government based on these principles.

Liberal

Liberal politics is based on the concept of a purely secular government. Since it is based on a naturalistic worldview foundation that does not recognize the existence of a transcendent power or purpose, politics is necessarily focused completely on a temporal outcome that promotes the ultimate goal of the natural order – the survival of the species. As such, the aim of politics is to organize society in ways that are seen to promote this end. The focus, then, is on the interests of the collective rather than on the individual. Since a communal mentality is the governing principle of society, politics is best expressed through some type of collectivist political form. The most popular collectivist approaches in our current time include, progressivism, socialism, and communism. Various forms of dictatorship are also possible expressions of this political approach.

History

Conservative

The principal concept, in conservative thinking, for understanding the significance of history is found in the word *purpose*. Specifically, a conservative understanding of history is grounded in the purpose of God. Conservatives understand history as a purposeful, non-repetitive, sequence of events that began in God's creative activity, and is moving toward the accomplishment of the purpose for which He created it.

Liberal

Based on liberal concepts, history has no transcendent meaning because there is no transcendent existence. History becomes simply a record of the natural operation of the material universe. Mankind is seen to be progressing to higher levels through history, but this is strictly the result of evolutionary progression as a natural animal.

Economics

Conservative

Conservative economics is based in the concept of the stewardship of property. It begins with the understanding that God is the owner of His entire creation. Based on biblical teachings, the property individuals own is not really theirs. Rather, it is understood to be a sacred trust from God who is the ultimate owner. Individuals are responsible for managing the property in their care based on the desires and purposes of God.

Liberal

Liberal economics is based in Naturalism and operates on the principle of interventionism. A naturalistic understanding of economics begins with the belief that there is no supernatural existence. As a result, the only principles which exist to guide economics are those that society's leaders consider to be helpful in advancing the goals of human society. Based on naturalistic thought, the species (society) rather than the individual takes precedent. The tendency that emerges from that is an approach to doing economics which promotes the welfare of society above that of the individual. This generally involves some kind of central guidance by those who control the purse strings of society.

Chapter 2

What is Most Important to Know?

When people hear the terms "liberal" and "conservative," the immediate reaction tends to be related to politics. And while politics are certainly expressed through these terms, the belief foundations that they feed off of are so much broader. Life simply can't be separated out piece by piece that way. The same beliefs that are expressed in the political arena are also expressed in one's understanding of biology, theology, economics, sociology and on down the line.

Thus, the war that we observe being fought in the political arena between liberals and conservatives is not merely a political conflict. It is a spiritual war that engages every part of life. As such, ultimate victory in that war is only accomplished based on spiritual realities, not merely political ones.

People need a change of heart, not simply a change of politics. Creating a society that is capable of accomplishing the purposes of God requires spiritual change in individuals. Until people understand this larger perspective and begin becoming more diligent in working to create that kind of change, we will continue to see conflict dominate the culture.

Chapter 3

Worldview Foundations in Political Systems

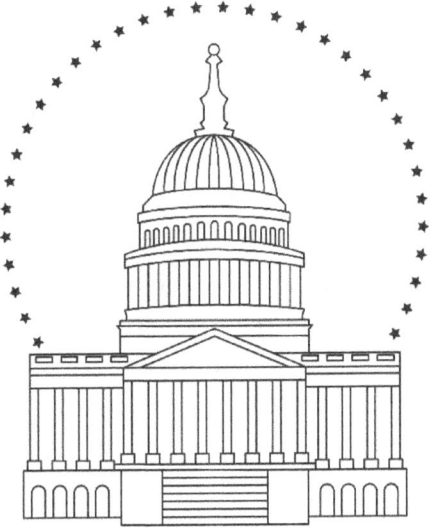

Many people identify their life philosophy with some political philosophy. That is, they identify a political philosophy that resonates with them, for whatever reason, and they build their lives around it. I suppose there is some rationality in that, but it is only partly rational.

The real issue that must be faced, especially for Christians, is that there is a set of beliefs that underlie every political philosophy. And unless those underlying beliefs are identified and compared to biblical beliefs, it is very possible for one to end up advocating for policies that run counter to God and His purposes. It is not sufficient to simply like a set of beliefs because it "feels right." It is critical for individuals to identify their reason for accepting a particular political philosophy, then compare that to what God has revealed about those beliefs in His revelation.

What we want to do here is to, first of all, identify the foundational beliefs of several of the major political philosophies that are prominent in modern society. After that, we will set that aside and look at the foundational beliefs that are expressed in the Bible. At that point, we will be in a position to compare the political philosophies with the biblical beliefs. With that, we will be able to see where the various political philosophies agree with, or diverge from, biblical teachings.

Conservative

When it comes to political discussions, the term conservative covers a lot of territory. Not only that, different people latch onto and promote different parts of the conservative label. Thus, one person's conservatism may not correspond completely to another's. Because of that, it is nearly impossible to pin it down completely. But it is possible to at least give a broad explanation and see where the general principles come from.

In broad terms, the word conservative does not represent political notions at all. It is the idea of holding on to what is traditional. As such, what is conservative in one context may be entirely different in another. So to deal with conservatism, it is necessary to first determine what a particular traditional point of view looks like.

In looking at political conservatism in American society, we must look back to America's founding to find the traditional notions modern conservatives are looking to retain. In modern political discussions, this typically gets divided into three parts. It is often called the three legged stool of conservatism. The three legs relate to three sets of values – social, national defense, and fiscal. These correspond, at least on some levels, to the ideals set forth in the Declaration of Independence of life (social values), liberty (safety/defense), and the pursuit of happiness (property/economics). Social conservatives promote traditional (biblical) values. National defense conservatives believe the military should be strong. And fiscal conservatives insists on a free market economy. Taking a comprehensive view, conservatives hold to all three legs.

What we are looking here to discover is where these values come from. It is pretty obvious that when it comes to conservative values in American culture, the ultimate source is the Bible.

The social values of the founders were based on the teachings of the Bible. In fact, the entirety of the structure of government was set up based on the belief that God exists and has revealed to mankind what is right and wrong. As such, the structure of the government and the laws of

Chapter 3

the land that were created were based on values that were expressed in the Bible.

As for the national defense arm, there is no specific biblical mandate for a strong military. However, there is the biblical principle that God has ordained the existence of government, and the purpose of government is to create an atmosphere where a nation can be secure, and where order can be maintained in society. While it is not the government's job to do the work of God in the world (that belongs to the church), God's purpose of order provides an atmosphere where His work can be done without hindrance. One part of keeping order relates to having a military that is strong enough to protect the nation and its people from outside invaders.

The fiscal arm of American conservatism also has its roots in biblical beliefs. The biblical principle that informs this area is stewardship. In biblical terms, everything ultimately belongs to God. However, God has appointed human beings to be stewards of His creation. His purpose is for individuals to manage the blessings He has placed in their care in order to accomplish His purposes. The founders used this concept to set up a system where individuals could own property and are responsible for how they use it (free enterprise).

So, as we can see, the principles which form the traditional notions about society that modern conservatives promote, came from the Bible. While many people who call themselves conservatives may not equally promote all three legs of the stool, and may not even promote the Christian faith in their own lives, the notions themselves do have biblical roots.

Liberal

The definition of the term "liberal" has changed significantly over the years in American society. Up until around 1900, it was a term which referred to an ideology that advocated for private property, an unhampered market economy, the rule of law, constitutional guarantees of freedom of religion and of the press, and international peace based on free trade. In modern times, though, these matters have become the domain of Conservatism while Liberalism has moved in a different direction.

Modern liberalism has come to be associated with ideas that do not hold with traditional American values, but with values that break away from tradition. In particular, they emerge from the beliefs of Naturalism.

Naturalism is the belief that the material universe, operating by natural laws, represents the entirety of reality. There is no God and, indeed, no supernatural existence at all. When applied to political ideology, the result of that kind of belief is that all laws, and other means of organizing society, must be created based on human reason. Rather than an emphasis on the individual, the emphasis is on the collective – the ultimate collective value being "the survival of the species."

Chapter 3

When it comes specifically to the expression of political goals and means, the "law of the jungle" rules. Since there is understood to be no God, and, indeed, no values from any transcendent source, the ruling force becomes the individuals who are able to acquire enough power to impose their will. It then becomes their judgment that determines the best way to accomplish the "survival of the species." Typically, this approach to governing promotes a communal concept of property, a controlled economy, the rule of those who hold power, and a de-emphasis on individual liberty. The most prominent expressions of this kind of governing philosophy in modern society would be Socialism, Marxist Communism, and some form of totalitarian dictatorship.

Hybrids

The truth is, though, there is not a lot of pure conservatism or pure liberalism around. What we see most often are hybrids. These hybrids begin with the basic foundation of either Christian Theism or Naturalism, then pull ideas from other places to take some final form. This can be seen to some degree among some conservatives (as was alluded to above) who only emphasize one or two legs of the three-legged stool. But there are some more formalized hybrid belief systems, as well. At this point, it is not useful to get too detailed about this as our purpose is not to do an academic treatment, but to give a big picture sense of how this plays out.

Libertarian

In its essence, Libertarianism is the view that people have the right to live their lives any way they choose so long as it respects the rights of others. Libertarians tend to defend each person's right to life, liberty, and property. The primary focus is to favor freedom and oppose government action that attempts to promote either equality or order.

From a big picture point of view, Libertarianism is weighted toward Conservative ideas. It strongly argues for the implementation of conservative economic policy, and has a particularly strong bias in favor of interpreting the Constitution based on original intent. On the other hand, it is more liberal when it comes to social issues. Since Libertarians believe in personal freedom to an extreme, they believe that people ought to be able to live their lives pretty much any way they wish as long as it does not impose on the rights of others.

From a worldview perspective, the economic and constitutional notions of Libertarianism are founded upon the biblical concepts of stewardship and the idea that there is an objectively real and valid foundation upon which to base law and order. On the other hand, its view of social issues is more complex. The concepts of individual rights and personal freedom definitely have their roots in biblical morality. However, its view that it is possible for people to be completely autonomous concerning morality without affecting the order of society comes primarily from the liberal belief that there is no such thing as an objectively real morality. Thus, libertarians end up hybridizing

Chapter 3

Christian Theism and Naturalism to create their point of view.

Socialist & Progressive

While Libertarianism is a hybrid weighted toward conservatism, Socialism and Progressivism are weighted toward liberalism. Socialism is a political and economic approach to organizing society that promotes the notion that the state should own all the means of production and distribution. It advocates that everyone work for the government and it is the government's job to distribute the proceeds of that work as it sees fit. Progressivism, as it is conceived of in modern culture, has basically the same goals as Socialism, but seeks to get there in a progressive manner rather than simply switching immediately.

The goal of both is to improve human life by human effort. This point of view is based on the Naturalistic worldview belief that man can, by his own efforts, create a society that is just and fair.

In order to come to its ideals, though, there must be some definition of what justice and fairness means. Justice and fairness based on a naturalistic point of view does not have any kind of objective basis. In fact, even the very concept of justice and fairness are not inherent to naturalistic worldview presuppositions. Thus, Socialists and Progressives must borrow their moral beliefs from somewhere else.

In America, since the beliefs about morality emerged out of a historical context in which Christianity was the prior dominant belief, the ideas about justice and fairness that Socialism and Progressivism latched onto were Christian. In essence, what they did was to take these concepts and divorce them from their Christian worldview roots, and attach them to their new naturalistic systems. In this way, a hybrid belief system was created using both naturalistic and Christian theistic ideas.

Biblical

For Christians, the most important thing is not any kind of political expression. Rather, it is the biblical teaching. Political goals are completely subordinated to the purpose of God. In God's economy, ultimate goals are spiritual, not physical. God's purpose is for every person in the world to enter into a personal relationship with Him based on Christ's sacrificial death on the cross.

But that does not mean there is no value in political efforts. The Bible is very clear that God created government for a purpose, and that human beings should live life as good and faithful citizens. And just what is that purpose? It is to create a just and orderly society so that God's work can be effectively accomplished in the world. This does not imply that the government is to be the instrument for doing the work of God. Rather, it is to create an environment where justice and order prevail so that citizens can go about doing the work of God in a free and open society.

Of course, there is no system of government that is able to perfectly fulfill God's purposes. However, the founders of the American structure were able to create a system which provided the means for that to happen. This system was specifically built on principles that are unique to Christianity. These principles enshrined, as non-negotiable precepts, the rule of law, freedom of conscience, the value of life, and the priority of the individual. Based on these principles, everyone, regardless of their individual religious preferences, can live their lives as they see fit. It also provides a system of order which is both fair and just based on the definitions of fairness and justice that are expressed in the Bible. If any of these underlying principles are changed, an entirely different society necessarily emerges which does not allow for the kinds of rights and freedoms that are inherent in biblical values.

Where Biblical Teachings and Political Philosophies Diverge

Obviously, there is a certain amount of overlap between worldview beliefs and political philosophy. After all, every approach to politics emerges out of some belief about how reality is structured.

For some, there is actually no divergence whatsoever. The goals of the worldview are the same as the goals of the political philosophy.

When it comes to the Christian faith, though, there is a distinct separation. This divergence is not in the values and principles that guide it, but in the roles that are played by the various institutions of society.

The ultimate purpose of God, as revealed in Scripture, is for people to know Him in a personal relationship. He created the world and man in a way that can provide for that relationship. But the nature of the material world is such that the various institutions that operate in the world must have their own purposes, as well. For the institution of government, that purpose is to provide an environment for society that promotes order and justice. The reason for this purpose, in God's economy, is so that His work can be effectively accomplished in the world. It is not government's job to do His work – that is the work of the church. However, His purpose is that government create an environment where that can happen. So while there is a divergence of sorts, the purposes do overlap.

Where the overlap exists is that the government should create an environment of order and justice based on the values God has revealed. Using a different set of values does not provide that outcome. Different values promote a loss of liberty that inhibits the work of God in the world.

Where it All Ends

In the end, I believe everyone desires a utopian world. And most people look to political forces to create a means for that to happen. But not all value sets allow people to move toward that perfect outcome. What is necessary for movement in that direction is for there to put in place a set of transcendent values that are recognized and followed by the entirety of society.

In the entire history of the world, the only set of values that has ever been able to provide for the kind of liberty necessary to accomplish that goal are biblical values. To the degree politicians and political institutions recognize and follow that pattern, order and justice will prevail. To the degree they don't, chaos will ensue.

Part II
Politics and Values

Chapter 4

A Christian Worldview Perspective on Freedom

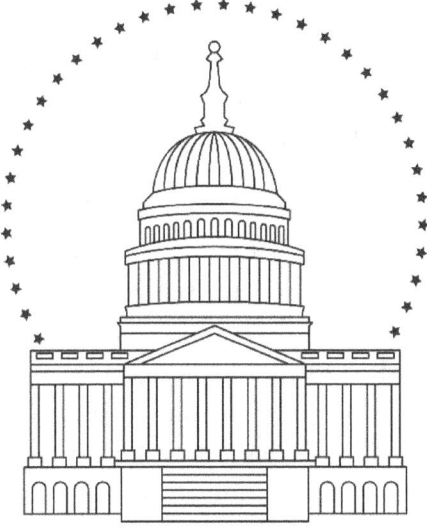

Freedom has a much deeper root than most people conceive. Usually when the topic of freedom is discussed, the context relates to a nation not being under the control of another, one class of people not being dominated by another class, or even an individual not being enslaved by a master. But those are only outward expressions of freedom.

In truth, authentic freedom's root is not in the outward expressions that we see in the culture. Rather, it is in the

Chapter 4

hearts of individuals. Freedom progresses from the individual to the culture, not the other way around.

Possible Worldview Perspectives on Freedom

A common belief in American culture is that many different kinds of beliefs can support freedom. However, that is simply not true. The only worldview system capable of actually producing authentic freedom is the one that represents the truth about reality – the Christian worldview. Let's look at this a little more carefully.

Those who hold to Naturalism (the belief that the natural universe operating by natural laws is all that exists) seek freedom, but have no way to even get at what that means. A naturalistic point of view doesn't even allow for the human spirit to exist as anything other than chemical, electrical, and biological functions. Thus, internal freedom can only be conceived of as feelings of personal satisfaction. As for freedom in the culture, a naturalistic point of view inevitably leads to a restriction of the freedom of the non-ruling class.

Animists can never be free as they are restricted to the rules of the universe (whatever that is). They must always be concerned with what pleases the spirits/gods, and they necessarily live in fear that they will misstep and create havoc in their own lives and in the lives of others.

Far Eastern Thought (pantheistic/monistic) believers are unable to be free as they believe their very existence in the material universe prevents it. There can be no freedom for them until the part of the life force that animates their physical existence escapes the bondage of their illusory material existence. To get freedom, they believe they must escape to the place where there is no personality and no consciousness.

Non-biblical Theism also does not produce freedom. True freedom can only be known within a relationship with God. And any representation of God that does not correspond to what the Bible teaches can only separate and isolate individuals from Him – and thus keep them disconnected from the one and only true source of freedom.

Freedom Begins in the Heart of the Individual

In its most basic form, true authentic freedom is rooted in the hearts of individual human beings. It is liberty from the power of guilt and sin.

In Galatians 5:1 we read,

> "It is for freedom that Christ has set us free. Stand firm, then, and do not let yourselves be burdened again by a yoke of slavery."

The focus here is on internal, not external freedom.

In this passage, the apostle Paul tells individual believers that since they have found this kind of internal freedom in Christ, they should be determined to remain free – to stand strong against the things that can enslave the heart. The things that enslave the heart are all material concerns related to worldly activities, personal habits, and religious practice.

The Progression of Freedom - Individual to Culture

As we have already noted, freedom does not start in the culture. It starts in the hearts of individuals. Then, when it has conquered the heart, it gets expressed through people's lives out in the culture.

When a person's heart is in bondage there are two places it tends to get expressed. The first expression is seen in the way it destroys the individual from the inside. Emotions such as hate, anger, pride, jealousy, and fear rob a person of joy in life, and can even lead to physical and mental breakdown. The other expression is seen in the attempt to dominate other people.

In the workplace we see it in bosses who beat down those working under them. We also see it in politicians who stoop to unethical and selfish behavior, and in corporate executives who are willing to walk over others to advance their own careers. We see it in church leaders and members who needlessly or maliciously stir up controversy, and in situations where individuals literally enslave other people for their own profit. It is only when the hearts of individuals have become free from bondage that it is at all possible for there to be freedom in the culture.

What Freedom Is Not

There are numerous ways people conceive of freedom, and not all of them actually correspond to the true meaning of the word. Some think of freedom as the ability to just do anything they wish. However, freedom is not merely the living of life without accountability. It is very possible for people to have the means to live life according to their own selfish desires yet be slaves inwardly.

It is *not* freedom when an individual lives with broken relationships, loneliness, anger issues, unsatisfied greed, self-centeredness, and the like. Nor does authentic freedom legitimately relate to one's ability to exercise personal indulgence, to act without accountability or boundaries, or to exert power over others in order to dominate and control.

What Freedom Involves

Ultimately, true authentic freedom begins with putting aside personal sin (the root of internal bondage). From there it moves out into the life of the individual and is expressed as freedom of conscience. Finally, when enough of the citizenry know this kind of personal freedom, it is able to move out into the culture to create freedom from oppression. This is seen when all citizens have the ability to freely seek their own opportunities. It exists as the freedom to fail as well as to succeed.

For those who base their lives on non-biblical worldview platforms, understanding the foundational basis of

Chapter 4

freedom is nearly impossible. In the minds of most people, an understanding of freedom comes only from its material expression out in the culture. But this totally misses the true nature of reality.

True freedom is rooted in the hearts of individuals. Thus, it is very possible to be outwardly free yet still be a slave. It is also possible to be a slave outwardly yet be free inwardly.

True freedom begins when people are able to release the bondage of sin based on a personal relationship with God through Jesus Christ. That is of ultimate importance as we live our individual lives. If we want to see freedom in the world, it is necessary that the society be dominated by people who know true inward freedom. It is only when this exists that a society is able to have a moral environment that supports authentic external freedom.

Chapter 5
Human Rights, Constitutional Rights, and Christian Rights

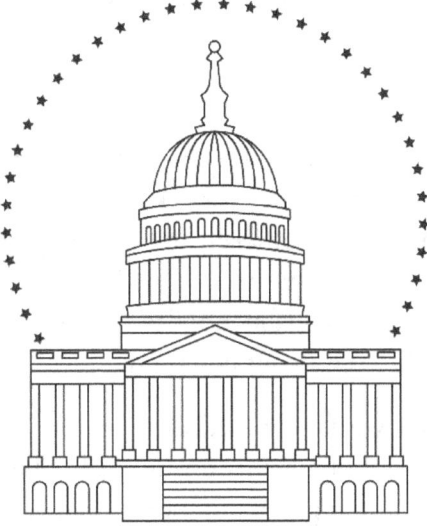

In 2011, U.S. District Judge Clark Waddoups, in a polygamy case, handed down a decision that a provision in Utah law forbidding cohabitation with another person violated the First Amendment right to freedom of religion. Freedom of religion, you say? What could the striking down of a cohabitation law possibly have to do with freedom of religion?

Well, it seems that this ruling came as a result of a lawsuit by the Brown family who are polygamists. They starred in

Chapter 5

a TLC reality TV show called "Sister Wives." It is a show about a real polygamist family of fundamentalist Mormons who share their life with viewers through the show. The problem is, polygamy is illegal in Utah.

The state of Utah originally instituted their cohabitation laws in 1890 because they wanted statehood, and the other states would not allow them into the union unless they abandoned their official acceptance of polygamy. Until then, the Mormon church fully accepted the practice (and it is still, actually, a part of their scriptures). In Utah, they don't issue multiple marriage licenses, so polygamous families consist of one officially married couple and the rest of the wives simply cohabit with the man. The implementation of cohabitation laws was the way the state of Utah tried to stamp out polygamy.

When the Brown family filed their lawsuit in July 2011, they did so believing their constitutional rights were being infringed. After filing the suit, they fled Utah because they were afraid of prosecution. They lived in Las Vegas until this ruling came down which removed the threat of arrest. The next step, of course, is to have polygamy itself accepted in law as legal marriage.

So now we see the next maneuver in the evolution of the very basis for understanding what is legal in America. If polygamous behavior is a human right, then the banning of it in law must also be unconstitutional. In other words, by simply changing the definition of a word, the legality of previously illegal activities can become legal.

And what's next after that? If polygamous behavior is a human right and a constitutional right, then any objection to it must be wrong. And so the progression goes.

These days, it seems that everyone is concerned that their rights not be infringed, and people are claiming "rights" in all kinds of ways. Homosexual marriage has already been deemed legal by the Supreme Court (in contradiction to the way this has been viewed for the entire previous history of the nation) simply by changing the definition of the word marriage.

There is a problem, though. Accepting immoral behavior based on changing the definition of words changes not only specific laws, but actually alters the very philosophical (worldview) basis upon which the concept of human rights, and American constitutional rights, was established. And if you change the philosophical basis, it changes the way you must evaluate all laws that deal with the word with the changed definition.

What used to be illegal and wrong automatically becomes legal and right without ever changing any laws. Old laws are just declared invalid by judges. Change the definition of marriage and all of sudden non-marriage behavior comes under the protection of marriage laws.

Another example relates to freedom of speech and religion. These ideas used to have very specific meanings based on the philosophical reasoning of the founders. But with a simple arbitrary change in the definition of a few words, freedom of speech is changed to mean certain speech is

Chapter 5

okay and other not okay. Additionally, freedom of religion comes to mean certain religious expressions are okay and not others.

Those who are advocating for this change in the philosophical foundation of our national culture make the claim that the religious concepts of the founders no longer fit a nation that is now religiously pluralistic. They believe we need a way of implementing laws that have no religious foundation at all. The problem is, there is no such thing. What they tout as a secular foundation for law is actually just that of a different religious faith. It is simply the replacement of one set of religious beliefs and values for another.

As for the polygamists, they say current law tramples on their right to marry who they want. What they don't realize is that by changing what currently exists, they are imposing their desires on others in a way that tramples their rights. In this case, children have a human right to be raised in a stable home that reflects the way reality is actually structured.

When God created humanity, he did it in a particular way. That way was designed with marriage being the union of one man and one woman for life. It is the way that a man and a woman can have the most fulfillment in their own lives, and it is the arrangement that is most advantageous for the raising of children.

There is no doubt that there are bad heterosexual marriages where spouses and/or children are abused. But this is not a problem with the institution, it is a problem with individuals within the institution living life in opposition to God's leading. But when you make the leap and redefine the nature of marriage to mean something that is outside of God's plan (whether you are talking about cohabitation, homosexual marriage, adultery, divorce, or polygamous marriage), problems begin shooting off the charts – everything from child and partner abuse, to pornography, to poverty, to substance abuse, to poor performance in school, to gender identification problems, and the list goes on and on. All of this happens with the simple redefinition of a word. It happens because these alternative arrangements literally operate against the actual way God structured reality to exist.

Ultimately, the issue is not about human rights or constitutional rights. It is about right and wrong. There is a way reality is actually structured and it is based on the way God created it. And we can know what that is because God revealed it to us in Scripture.

When it comes to operating in human culture, the concepts of human rights and constitutional rights are important. They provide the framework for establishing right morality in the world and for interacting with others in society in a free and orderly manner.

But human rights and constitutional rights, themselves, must by necessity be based on something concrete. Either the basis is the actual structure of reality (that which is revealed in the Bible) or something else, which is not.

Chapter 5

The truth is, human beings are sinners who truly deserve eternal separation from God. In spite of that, God loves us with such a great depth of love that moved Him to come to earth as a human person and give Himself as a sacrifice for the purpose of taking care of our sin problem. He did this *not* because we have a right to it, but because He loves us. And, based on that love, He determined to show us mercy. As such, rather than demanding rights from Him, we ought to be so grateful for His love and mercy toward us that we humbly and willingly give our lives – every part of our lives – to Him. That giving of our lives should be expressed by giving Him the one thing He wants out of us – our loving devotion back to Him.

Human rights and constitutional rights in America ultimately emerged out of the very character of God Himself. Unfortunately, in our day, the definitions of these concepts are being perverted in ways which create behavior in society that is, itself, perverted.

The only cure for this is to know God. Christians should recommit themselves to spread this cure to all they know. It is only when people know Christ that they will even understand the true meaning of human rights and constitutional rights.

Chapter 6

Are Christian Values Necessary for Freedom in America?

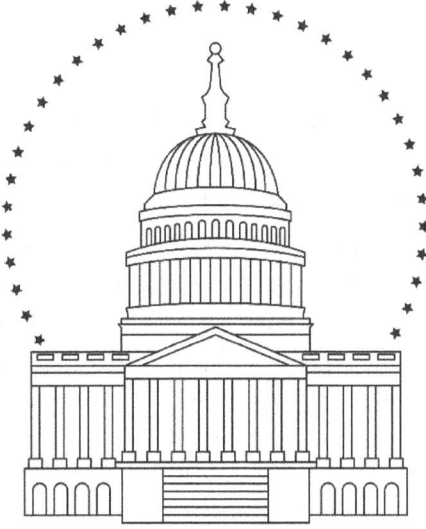

Not too long back, the Home and Garden Television network (HGTV) announced its decision to pull the plug on an upcoming real estate reality show. This show was about twins David and Jason Benham – two guys who help families create their dream home from "fixer-uppers." And why was the show pulled? It had absolutely nothing to do with the content of the show.

Chapter 6

Rather, it was because of the private beliefs of the two stars. They were accused by gay rights activists of being anti-gay and pro-life because they dared express their biblical beliefs out loud – in their private life. Because of the demands of radical homosexual rights activists, the network caved and pulled the show. This is pretty much the same thing that the A & E Network tried to do with Phil Robertson of Duck Dynasty fame.

Then, there is the case of former Mozilla Firefox CEO Brendan Eich. He is recognized as, literally, a genius in the internet tech world and was a perfect person to become the head of this company. However, very shortly after he was selected, the company was pressured by radical homosexual activists to kick him out because he made a monetary contribution to the California pro natural marriage amendment effort back in 2008.

And these two headlines are only the tip of the iceberg when it comes to the pressure to eliminate Christian values from the public square. There are numerous recent headlines where the immoral speech and actions of individuals are accepted and celebrated, and others where the private expression of traditional values leads to public sanction. These various headlines include such topics as: personal speech (an NBA team owner was forced to sell his franchise based on illegally taped bigoted remarks he made in the privacy of his own home), political thuggery (the U.S. Attorney General who refused to prosecute law breakers or even follow the law himself), destruction of economic opportunity (the implementation of public policies based on a political philosophy that makes it easy for people to avoid personal responsibility), sexual immorality (the normalization of polygamy, homosexuality, adultery, and fornication), and abortion (the devaluing of life for personal convenience). And honestly, the list could go on and on.

In modern society, it is *not* okay to hold certain opinions if they are deemed to be politically incorrect by certain cultural elites. On the other hand, it is okay for those with political or social power to make up their own morality and force it on the entire society using brute force. And in our world today, the rules governing these things can change over time based on the beliefs of social influencers, regardless of what the law says.

Basically, the rule of law has been set aside. What was right can become wrong and vice versa, based purely on the personal beliefs of those in power. For people who believe in the rule of law and freedom of conscience, it is disturbing to witness individuals being persecuted for their opinions and driven out of business and/or out of the public square.

The political correctness that is behind all of the intolerance mentioned above is a function of a naturalistic worldview. Naturalism is the belief that the material universe, operating by natural laws is all that exists. There is no God or any kind of supernatural existence. As such, Naturalists believe that everything, in all of reality, can be accounted for by natural means.

Chapter 6

As it relates to moral judgements, since there is no God to reveal any kind of transcendent moral law, the only place morality can come from is the opinions of individual human beings. And based on that belief set, morality is determined by those who hold the power to enforce their beliefs – the law of the jungle.

So, here is the bottom line: Some set of worldview beliefs will dominate a society. As America was founded on Christian worldview beliefs, the values that have dominated American society for most of its history have been Christian values. This does not mean that everyone in the society was a Christian, or even agreed with all Christian values. In fact, far from it.

What it does mean, though, is that a certain set of Christian values that relate to governmental structure and the exercise of power in society were commonly accepted by virtually the entirety of the population. It is these biblical worldview values that have defined America's uniqueness. These values include:

1. Freedom of conscience: Freedom of conscience means people are free to follow any religion or belief set they want. It means individuals are allowed to live their lives and speak their opinion in the way they personally choose without fear of being persecuted or marginalized by legal authorities (assuming, of course, that their actions don't infringe the rights of others).

2. Equal justice before the law: This means there is no arbitrariness in the legal system. Everyone, regardless of their station in life, will be judged based on the same set of laws.

3. Sanctity of life: The principle of the sanctity of life refers to the belief that no innocent human life, regardless of its immediate state, shall ever be taken.

4. Personal responsibility: The value of personal responsibility expresses the belief that every person is responsible for his or her own life. As such, society should be set up to allow people to succeed or fail based on their own efforts and abilities. There should be no special privilege or hindrances placed on any group or individual that would infringe this principle. For those who need special help, some kind of accommodation should be implemented, but not in a way that violates the larger principle.

5. Biblical sexual morality: The family is the most important institution for the promotion of stability in society. The promotion of biblical sexual values strengthens this institution. That is not to say that deviant sexual behavior should necessarily be criminalized. However, it should never be accepted and celebrated in law either. At the same time, all laws and social systems that strengthen the traditional family should be promoted.

In recent years, these unique values have been challenged by opposing values that have emerged from a naturalistic worldview. The result has been the downward spiral of American society. The result is:

Chapter 6

1. Societal rules (laws, mores and folkways) based on power and personal preference: Freedom of conscience and biblical morality are replaced by political correctness and personal permissiveness. This leads to hedonistic indulgence and repression against anyone who thinks or acts contrary to the beliefs of the cultural power brokers.

2. Arbitrariness in legal matters: When the rule of law is *not* strictly observed, lawlessness becomes the order of the day. Laws that are disliked or deemed "unfair" by those who are charged with enforcing them can simply be ignored.

3. Devaluation of life: In naturalistic thought, the value of life is based on the personal beliefs of the cultural and political elite. Economic considerations and personal convenience trump individual lives when it comes to deciding who should live or die, or what kind of life certain classes of people are consigned to live.

4. Social control: Using naturalistic presuppositions, equality of outcome generally trumps equality of opportunity. In other words, it is deemed proper that everyone in society should have the same benefits and privileges regardless of the effort they put forth in life. Unfortunately, this never has and never will create an environment where true equality exists. To implement this, there must, by necessity, be a ruling class. This ruling class will always find a way to exempt itself from the negative impact of this approach, and, as a result, will always be in a position to control the masses.

5. Sexual freedom: Since in Naturalism there is no objective moral standard, literally anything goes when it comes to sexual morality. There is no such thing as any kind of inherently wrong sexual activity. This ends up having a devastating effect on the family. And when the traditional family is broken down, the glue that holds society together disintegrates. The result is higher crime, greater poverty, lower education levels, more people dependent on government assistance, less personal initiative, lower employment and wages, and a whole host of other physical, emotional, and mental problems.

The truth is, the headlines at the beginning of this chapter are the natural result of the naturalistic point of view that dominates modern society. Most polls taken in recent years show an increasing sense that the American public believes we are headed down the wrong road. And that wrong road is quite easy to identify.

It is the road of naturalistic worldview beliefs, and there is only one way to change the direction. It is to intentionally move back to the Christian principles that are our heritage. And the only way to do that is to elect leaders who believe in those values.

The only problem is, too many of those who live in modern society want to hybridize their beliefs. They want to have their proverbial cake and eat it too. They want the good results that come from a society built on biblical values, but don't want to be put in a position where they themselves are held accountable for personal decisions and activities that reflect anti-biblical behavior. With this kind of hybridized belief system dominant in society, it becomes difficult, if not impossible, to determine where the line should be drawn concerning what is morally acceptable.

People want freedom of conscience for themselves but are willing to shut down the speech of those who express contrary opinions. People say they want equal justice under the law but are willing to allow elected officials to selectively enforce the law, or even ignore laws they don't agree with. People say they support life, but are willing to allow some life to be considered of lesser or no value, and to be enslaved or even killed.

People say they want to help those who are down and out, but find it easier to consign them to a life of dependence on government handouts than to make the effort to provide opportunities for them to grow and flourish. People say they want social stability, but not to the extent that they are willing to accept and live by the kind of moral beliefs that are necessary for that to happen. The problems we see in modern society exist solely because the values inherent in a naturalistic worldview are so widely accepted by the population at large. Thus, the desire for the recognized benefits of biblical moral values are set aside for the pleasures of sinful indulgence and/or temporary expediency.

Ultimately it is *not* new laws or new technology that will be our nation's salvation (if salvation is to come at all). Laws that are based on arbitrary values, or which are not enforced in order to indulge selfishness and sensuality, are no laws at all. Technology that has the potential for good can also be used for evil – and will be when those using it have evil hearts.

No, the only thing that can put our nation back on the right track is a population that recognizes what values are good and right, AND is willing to put aside evil and actually implement what is right. A change in direction to reverse the evil and perversion that has become part and parcel of modern society only comes from changed hearts. And changed hearts only come from acceptance of the good news of the gospel of Jesus Christ.

Chapter 7

Can America Be Moral Without God?

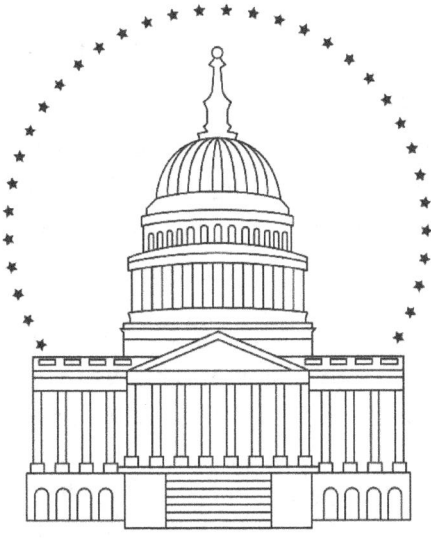

John Adams, one of America's founding fathers, delivered a message on October 11, 1798, to the Officers of the First Brigade of the Third Division of the Militia of Massachusetts. In that message he said:

> "Our Constitution was made only for a moral and religious people. It is wholly inadequate to the government of any other."

Now why would he say such a thing? Over the last few years various Atheist groups around the country have been

Chapter 7

putting up billboards to promote their belief. One of them reads: I can be good without God.

But the question emerges, "What possible criteria could an Atheist use to make such an assertion?"

Where Does Morality Come From?

I have had the opportunity, on numerous occasions, to have conversations with outspoken Atheists. At some point, we always seem to migrate to the topic of morality. What usually happens is that the Atheist makes some kind of claim to be a good, moral person.

But here is the problem: Morality has to be built on something. It is a designation that must be understood in relation to some standard. When considering the concept of morality based on Christianity, the standard is pretty straightforward – the teachings of the Bible. But what is the standard for Atheists? That is much more nebulous.

Atheists don't believe God exists, so there is no one outside the material universe to establish any kind of objective moral standard. That only leaves human beings to set the standard themselves. So where should they get it from? For Atheists, there are not too many possibilities.

One of the more common approaches they use is to invoke "the common good." That is, what best provides for the survival of the species or the community. Unfortunately, this is a rather arbitrary way to define morality. Someone has to make that determination, and it is usually the ones in positions of power. That means, those who attain power in society have the ability to impose their beliefs and views on everyone else based on what they believe is good for the collective. In that case, it doesn't really matter what individuals think.

Another common approach is to invoke personal preference. This allows individuals to make up their own morality. The biggest drawback with this is that there is inherent conflict between people who prefer different approaches. Ultimately, it still comes down to who has the ability to impose their will on others.

One other possibility is for Atheists to borrow their morality from somewhere else. Those who claim "I can be good without God," generally borrow their sense of morality from some religious system – frequently from the Christian faith. They often identify such actions as killing, stealing, lying (and other sins that are revealed in the Bible) to be evil.

It is also not unusual for them to invoke the golden rule (do unto others as you would have them do unto you) as a positive standard. The only problem is, there is no objective reason for them to identify any of these things as either good or bad. For them, it is an arbitrary judgement.

America's Historical Moral Foundation

No matter the situation, there will always be some standard of morality that dominates a society. There is always some default orthodoxy. In America, the default is Christian Theism. This is the foundation the founders used as they

Chapter 7

set up the nation's various institutions. The moral beliefs they operated from were those taught in the Bible.

This brings into focus John Adam's statement quoted at the beginning of this chapter, where he made it clear that only moral or religious people would be able to keep the Constitution in play – as atheists or immoral people would need something with more enforcement power. Evidently John Adams felt a Constitutional democracy would only work with a moral populous.

But the moral beliefs, by themselves, don't give us the full picture. There are different ways to evaluate and follow moral teachings. As we look at the implementation of morality in American society, there are two basic ways it can be, and has been, expressed – internal and external.

The internal expression is based on one's personal relationship with God. Of course, you can't get away from the need to have an intellectual understanding of biblical teachings concerning what is right and wrong. That said, the motivation for actually living by what the Bible teaches is a desire to please a personal God who is known in a personal relationship.

The other possible expression is external. This approach is also based on a belief that biblical teachings are right. But the motivation for living by them is impersonal rather than personal.

A person can go this route without even knowing a personal relationship with God. All they need to know is a list of rules that are derived from the Bible. The reason for choosing to legalistically follow the Bible, rather than some other set of rules, can be quite varied.

Some do it because that is the way they were raised and don't know any different. Others do it because they see the quality of the rules and believe this is better than other ways. The possible motivations are, literally, as varied as the number of people who follow this approach.

The Drift

To understand where American culture currently resides, it is helpful to trace the flow of cultural beliefs. Of course, this is, by necessity, a very generic explanation as there is no particular moment in time when American culture moved from one stage to another. It began, basically, in one place, and has ebbed, flowed, and trended to where it is now.

The true essence of the Christian faith is not a set of moral regulations. Rather it is a personal relationship with a personal God. The principles used in the founding of American society were derived specifically from the Bible by people who knew this kind of relationship. When principles come from this source, the rules of society take on a very unique quality.

People don't follow them because "these are the rules." Rather, they recognize biblical teachings as the way God wants things to be. And, because they love God, they desire to please him by living in ways that correspond to the

Chapter 7

"rules." In other words, adherence to societal principles (laws) is based on an internal desire to be obedient to God rather than on a legalistic adherence to rules.

Over time, the principles became institutionalized and people came to live by them simply because "these are the rules." Unfortunately, as time passed, the percentage of people who followed the principles because of a personal relationship with God declined. At some point the majority still believed in and followed the "rules," but the motivation was external rather than internal. When that happens, the object of loyalty changes from God to the rules themselves, or to the nation.

The next step occurs when a generation comes along that begins to question the legitimacy of the rules. Without a personal connection to God, the rules are not tethered to anything absolute. They become just one possibility among many for regulating society. At this stage, various groups begin advocating for a different set of rules – which are inevitably established on an entirely different moral foundation.

Finally, when a majority is established who don't like the founding principles, the rules are changed in a way that sets aside the old foundation and establishes a new one. At that point, power and personal desire become the foundational principles that govern society rather than God's revelation. And this is, essentially, where American society has gone.

Back to the Beginning

So, we are now back to the original question: Can America Be Moral Without God? Of course it can … if you define morality based on human opinion. But there is such a thing as an objective way reality exists, and that objective reality includes the God who is revealed in the Bible. Beyond that, this God has revealed Himself – not just in laws He wants us to follow, but as an actual person with whom we are able to have a personal relationship.

The truth is, America cannot be moral without God because, in an objective sense, morality is based on a relationship with Him. If He does not exist, no objectively real morality exists – only people's personal conception of it. Or, if a person does not have a relationship with God, they are not aligned with the true morality that does exist.

Morality is, at its most fundamental level, tied to a personal relationship with God. It is essentially an internal set of beliefs that are expressed externally. People can do acts that imitate true morality, but unless the internal element is present, the morality is an empty shell. Those who claim they can be moral without God simply do not understand the true meaning of what it means to be moral. In its most profound sense, people cannot be moral without God!

Chapter 8

What Do 21st Century American Values Look Like?

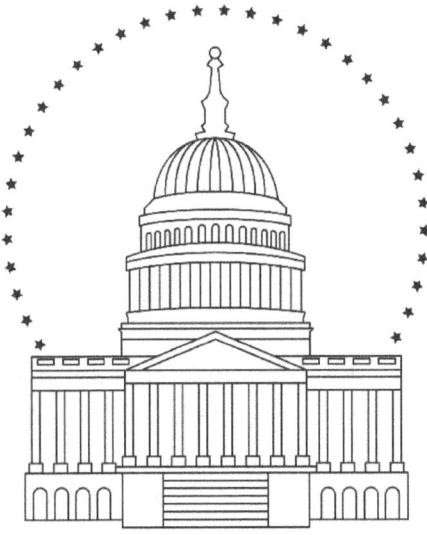

The Nature of the Values War

There are more than two value systems at play in modern culture, but there are two that are far and away the most prominent. These two value systems emerge out of two different worldview foundations.

The first value system is based on biblical Theism and corresponds to what is generally called conservative values. It is the worldview system upon which American society was founded. It was dominant in society from the time of America's founding until around the 1960s.

The second value system is based on Naturalism and corresponds to what is generally called liberal values. This is the worldview system that took over dominance in society around the 1960s, and has increased in its prominence since that time.

Biblical Theism is belief in the God of the Bible who has revealed Himself, His ways, and His will. As such, the values and morals which emerge out of it are those that are found in the Bible. The basic foundation of this approach is based on a belief in absolutes when it comes to moral teachings.

Naturalism, on the other hand, believes that there is no such thing as a supernatural reality. With that as a starting place, there can be no God to reveal right morality. It is entirely up to human beings to determine what should be right and wrong in human society. The approach for understanding morality is based on relativism. What is right and wrong are founded purely upon what individuals and societal consensus make it to be. This can change over time based on contemporary circumstances.

In order to grasp more concretely how this plays out in American culture, it is helpful to compare some of the primary values of biblical Theism and Naturalism as they are played out in society. Let's look at the contrast between conservative and liberal values.

Conservative Values (Based on Christian Theism)

Man Is Essentially Sinful - The belief, based on a biblical understanding of the nature of mankind, that societal constraints must be in place to temper the effects of sin.

Natural Law - The belief that there are inherent rights conferred by God.

Constitutional Authority - The belief that there is an overarching, authoritative legal framework that is the ultimate foundation for all other laws. This corresponds to the biblical concept of an authoritative document given by God.

Free Enterprise - The belief, based on biblical teachings, that individuals should work hard and be rewarded for their labor.

Individual Property Ownership - The belief, based on the biblical concept of stewardship and the priority of the individual, that individuals should hold personal property and be responsible to God for its use.

Freedom of Religion - The belief, based on the biblical concept that human beings are free will creatures created in the image of God, that individuals should make life decisions based on freedom of conscience.

Chapter 8

Federalism - The belief, based on the biblical concept of man as a sinner and on the priority of the individual over the collective, that governmental power ought to be decentralized, with power also shared at more local levels.

Separation of Powers - The belief, based on the biblical concept that human beings are sinful and that concentrated power in the hands of only a few people allows their moral weakness to disadvantage the population at large, that political power ought to be diluted.

Liberal Values (Based on Naturalism)

Man Can Build Utopia on Earth - The belief, based on the concept of naturalistic evolution, that man has already evolved to a higher form than other animal creatures and will continue on that path, that social engineering can enhance the evolution of the goodness of man.

Positive Law - The belief that man-made laws are responsible for bestowing upon, or removing, specific privileges from an individual or group. There is no God, so humans must make this determination for themselves.

Human Authority - The belief, based on naturalistic concepts, that the highest authority is man. Those in power positions in society are tasked with creating and changing law based on their perception of current circumstances.

Economic Collectivism - The belief, based on naturalistic presuppositions, that human survival is the highest value, and equal distribution of resources best promotes that in society.

Collective Ownership of Property - The belief, based on the naturalistic concept of the survival of the species and the priority of the collective, that corporate ownership of property best promotes the interests of society.

Individual Religious Belief Is Subservient to the Collective - The belief, based on the naturalistic concept that human beings are naturally evolved animal creatures, that governmental leadership is best able to decide what is best for the survival of the collective.

Centralized Federal Authority - The belief, based on the naturalistic concept of the priority of the collective, that concentrated political power most effectively promotes the survival of social groupings.

Concentration of Power - The belief, based on the naturalistic concept that the collective has priority over the individual, that centralized political power is best able to promote the survival of society.

Chapter 8

Fighting the Culture War in Our Lives

Interestingly, there is a large percentage of the population that mixes and matches these values to create their own personal philosophies of life, and their own value systems. However, this inevitably creates a situation where those individuals end up holding values that are internally contradictory.

Christians, on a personal level, constantly fight this battle. People consciously affirm biblical values, yet often find themselves struggling to put aside acts which represent values that come from another source. This is the struggle we all face as we seek to overcome and defeat sin in our lives. And make no mistake about it, this is a Christian's first priority. Unless we win the battle on a personal level, we will never see the influence of God's righteousness expressed in society.

The only way to truly win this battle in our lives is to acknowledge the Bible as the plumb line and work diligently to conform our lives to its standard. To do that, it is necessary to be brutally honest about the values we hold, and to consciously make changes in the areas we see deviance. This is not an easy thing to do. To begin with, it is often difficult to even see the places in our lives where we stray. Add to that our struggle to overcome the selfishness and pride that makes us *not* want to change, and the battle is on.

It is certainly possible to conform our lives and our thinking to what God desires, but it definitely requires great effort. Unfortunately, this is the nature of salvation. Not only must we make that first decision to invite Christ into our lives (justification), we must also live out our salvation in daily life (sanctification). As we do, we will increasingly conform our thinking to God's way. And as we do that, we will live those values out in every part of our lives.

But the battle does not end with the individual. The struggle that exists in individuals gets played out in society, as well. Just as we struggle within ourselves to gain personal alignment, so, society does the same.

There are those who think that we should not take this battle into society – that we ought to only focus on the personal side. But the truth is, the battle is already raging, and the influences of society are a big part of the struggle we face as individuals. And this not only applies to us, but to our children and our neighbors. If we allow unmitigated sin to run rampant in society, what we see is not only a generic degradation of the culture, but specifically that of our sons and daughters as they too are immersed in a society dominated by sexual immorality, substance abuse, and rampant hedonism.

As Christians, our number one goal is to keep ourselves in a right relationship with God on a personal, individual level. But that must be extended out beyond ourselves. We must also promote the values of God within society in a way that causes society to move toward biblical values.

Chapter 8

This creates the kind of environment where living rightly and sharing Christ's love would *not* bring the derision we see in our current circumstance in America today. However, as we attempt to do this, we will face opposition. Therefore, it is critical that we make the effort to get up to speed on how to best engage this struggle.

Part III
Faith and Actions

Concluding Observations

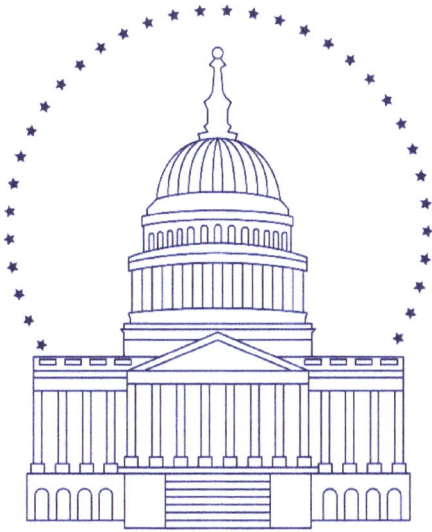

Our worldview beliefs form the basis for everything we think, say, and do – no matter what subject we are dealing with. That is eminently true for the topic of politics – the subject of this book. Our beliefs express how our religious views determine our very approach to politics – how we understand its meaning, the values we express in carrying out the political process, and the way we personally engage it.

As Christians, that means that our thoughts and deeds should always be guided by the teachings of the Bible – the source of our Christian worldview. In Scripture, God revealed Himself and His character to mankind. And in that revelation, He gave us guidance that we should seek to become like Him in every way – in our thoughts, words, and our actions. This biblical point of view corresponds to the way God intentionally created our material reality to work. When we allow ourselves to be guided by His revelation, our lives individually, and society as a whole, operate smoothly, just as God intended from the beginning. That should be the goal of every Christian.

Chapter 9

Citizenship Stewardship

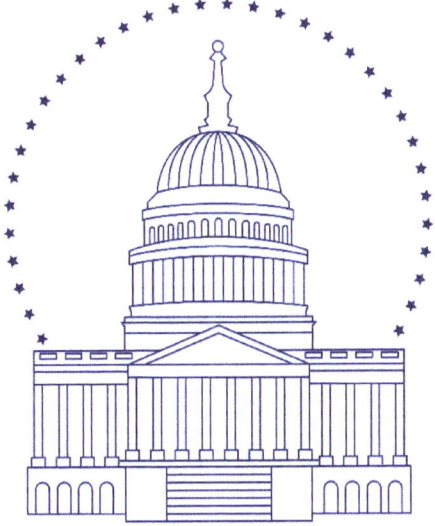

When it comes to any kind of political involvement, the process can be messy and unpleasant. Sadly, that very fact is often used by Christians as an excuse for not engaging the political process at all. But there are many parts of life that are messy and unpleasant. If we avoided our responsibilities in every part of life that can be characterized that way, we would be dropping out of a lot of things.

In fact, our thinking should be just the opposite. Our example should be Jesus Himself. He didn't avoid coming

Chapter 9

to earth because dealing with humans was messy and unpleasant. Instead, He stepped out of paradise and dropped Himself right into the middle of the mess in order to help us get out of it. We should be willing to do the same to help others.

But beyond that, there is another reason we should become politically engaged. We should do it because we have an actual responsibility from God. Christians in America are God's stewards of their elected representatives. We need to vote for people who hold Christian values, then observe their service to make sure they are representing us rightly.

In biblical days, the types of government that were most prominent were various forms of dictatorship – whether it was run by a king or an emperor. Under that kind of system, regular citizens were "subjects" and did not have much of an opportunity to impact the operation of government. In that circumstance, the Bible teaches that individuals are to obey God above any earthly ruler, but at the same time to be as obedient as possible to the ruling authorities in order that societal order may be maintained.

American society, though, was not set up to operate based on rulers. In America we have a representative government. The rulers are the people who elect others to represent them in government. As such, it is not the principle of obedience to rulers that is most important, but that of stewardship.

God is the owner of all things, but on earth He has made man His stewards (managers). Since political representatives are responsible to the citizens for their work, it becomes an individual's stewardship responsibility to manage this element of God's creation based on His will. Faithful citizens must monitor their representatives 'work and provide feedback and direction. If the representatives are not representing well, it is the responsibility of the citizens to replace them with different people who will.

While the process is the same for every citizen, the motivation for doing this is unique for Christians. We don't become politically active simply because the government is set up that way, but because we have a responsibility before God. As such, it is not just the act of selecting a representative that is important, but the kind of representation we promote, as well.

As Christian citizens, our primary responsibility is to elect representatives who will be faithful in carrying out particular principles God has revealed in the Bible. This does not in any way imply that believers are to elect people who will set up a theocracy. Rather, it is an admonition to elect representatives who are honest, full of integrity, and who will create, implement, and enforce laws that are consistent with the values of life and liberty that God has revealed in Scripture.

As we get down to real life where actual policy is created, there are many specific policy matters that come into play. When it gets to these specifics, even Christians may disagree about some of them. But we should never disagree about the values themselves, and we need to make sure our representatives do hold Christian values. The policy decisions they make ultimately emerge out of their values.

Two Primary Sources of Values in America

In modern American culture, there are primarily two competing sources for the values we see in the public square. These sources produce very different values and, thus, different ways of understanding what is right and wrong. The two are Naturalism and Christian Theism.

Naturalism is the belief that there is no such thing as a supernatural reality – no God and nothing outside of the material universe. Since Naturalists don't believe in the existence of God, it is impossible for their values to have a source outside of humanity. Thus, there are no absolutes to base morality upon. All morality is, by necessity, based on a relative foundation. That is, those in power personally evaluate any given situation and determine what they believe to be the best course based on their own beliefs.

Christian Theism, on the other hand, is the belief that there is a transcendent God who is the creator of the material universe. More specifically, it regards the God of the Bible to be that One true God. And the teachings He has revealed in the Bible form the basis for the values that reflect what is morally right.

What Are the Particular Values Christians Should Promote?

There are, of course, many values that are dealt with in the Bible, and politicians should use all of them as the starting point for developing public policy. That said, there are three that are foundational: life, family, and truth. There is a way God has created the world, and mankind, to exist, and these three foundation stones are key.

Life

When God made His creation, the most valuable thing He created was living creatures. The life He created was an expression of His own very existence. Because it is so valuable, life should be regarded as of highest value.

But there is one form of life in particular that holds the most value of all – human life. That is because humans are living creatures who were actually created in God's image. Human beings, thus, have the personhood characteristics of God Himself. Thus, human life is of the highest value on planet earth.

Family

Beyond individual human life, the next important value that needs to be protected relates to the family. The family is the most fundamental expression of relationship that exists among humanity, thus, the fundamental unit upon which society is built. God established the union of one man and one woman as the foundation for all of the rest of human society. Anything that serves to break down this most important of institutions should be resisted.

Truth

The third critical value that needs to be protected is truth. Truth represents the way reality is actually structured, and is the very basis for the living of life. This affects what people believe, what they say, the relationships they engage and build, as well as the lifestyle they embrace.

How Values Affect Policy Decisions

As politicians do their work, they develop laws and policies that establish the societal environment everyone must live in. The policies themselves deal with every facet of life. But it must be remembered that the policies are not the root, they are the flower.

In other words, policies are established upon something more fundamental. They are established upon a set of values. In order to develop laws and policies that are just and right, they must be founded upon the values God has revealed to be the right ones – life, family, and truth as they are expressed in the Bible.

There are many issues that humans in society must wrestle with. It is up to elected officials to develop policy initiatives that value individual life, strengthen the nuclear family, and promote truth. Some of the areas where politicians must develop policy include (but are not limited to):

About The Author:

Freddy Davis is the president of MarketFaith. He is the author of numerous books and has a background as an international missionary, pastor, radio host, worldview trainer, and entrepreneur. Freddy is a popular speaker, particularly on the topic of worldview and its practical implications for the Christian life. He lives in Tallahassee, FL with his wife Deborah.

Other books by Freddy Davis

The Truth Mirage

Shattering the Truth Mirage

Assaulting the Truth Mirage

Can America Survive?

Christian Worldview Commentary Series:

- Gospel of John

- Romans
- Galatians, Ephesians, Philippians, Colossians
- 1, 2, 3, John & Jude

www.freddydavis.com

About MarketFaith Ministries:

You and your church could be on a transformative journey of faith with MarketFaith Ministries. In today's diverse and complex world, we understand the challenges Christians face. Our mission is to guide and empower you to live out your Christian faith with clarity and conviction in a world that is increasingly hostile to Christianity. Using our cutting-edge materials and comprehensive training, you will gain a profound ability to take Christ to what is now a massively pluralistic society. We can lead you to discover a renewed sense of purpose and confidence as you learn to authentically embody your faith and use that to make a positive impact in the world. Contact MarketFaith Ministries and let's partner together on a path that will lead to the growth of your church or business, and to a new level of spiritual depth for individual believers.

www.marketfaith.org

- ***Social Issues*** - homelessness, poverty, hunger, mental illness, abortion, healthcare

- ***Ethics and Morality*** - sexual practice, family structure, business integrity

- ***Biology*** - environmental stewardship, animal protection and safety, medical practices

- ***Law*** - rule of law, justice, fairness, citizen protection, church and state balance, conscience protections

- ***Politics*** - political integrity, legislative rules

- ***Economics*** - business practices, individual property rights

- ***Education*** - accurate information, equal educational opportunity

Different values promote different outcomes. So, whichever worldview values are dominant in a society are the ones that will be expressed in society. If people who hold values consistent with Naturalism are running the show, you will end up with policies that promote such things as abortion, doctor assisted suicide, alternative family structures, sexual deviance, radical environmentalism, attacks on Christian expression in the public square, unequal justice, an "ends justifies the means" political philosophy, public ownership of property, government control of the content of educational materials, and the like. You get these kinds of policies because they are consistent with naturalistic belief.

On the other hand, if the people pulling the levers of government have biblical values, you get policies that promote such things as life, stable families, the rule of law, equal justice for all, promotion of the welfare of the individual, and access to equal educational opportunity.

How Do We Do It?

There is one thing we must keep in the forefront as we engage our Christian citizenship responsibilities. Our reason for being good stewards is *not only* for the purpose of accomplishing temporal policy objectives. Policy can only create an environment. And, although the environment is important as it determines how much freedom citizens are able to have as they live life, nevertheless the shape of the environment is not the ultimate goal. The ultimate goal is to enter into and live in a relationship with God through Jesus Christ. The environment is critically important because it creates the opportunity for individuals to work for God in society to accomplish the goal. But it is not the goal itself.

When the focus is primarily on policy, the policies themselves become the most important thing. But NO policy can possibly be good if it is not rooted in good values. Even what seems like ought to be good policy will turn out bad if the values it is founded upon are not good.

As Christians, we have a responsibility before God to be good stewards of our citizenship. Since, in America, ultimate political power rests in the hands of the citizen, we have a responsibility to know the people we select to represent us in the political arena, and an equal responsibility to know how they are representing us. We need to know their beliefs before we vote for them.

We then need to follow their votes as they serve in order to make sure they are voting our values. If things seem to be amiss, we need to make contact and let them know we are watching. And if they do not represent well, we need to select a different representative – one who will vote the way they promised.

None of this can be done by a non-engaged person. So, Christians have a responsibility before God to be engaged in the political process as responsible stewards. If every believer would take this responsibility seriously, the environment of our nation would change radically, and we would find ourselves in a position to be more effective in furthering the work of God in the world.

Chapter 10

Should Christians Be Politically Active?

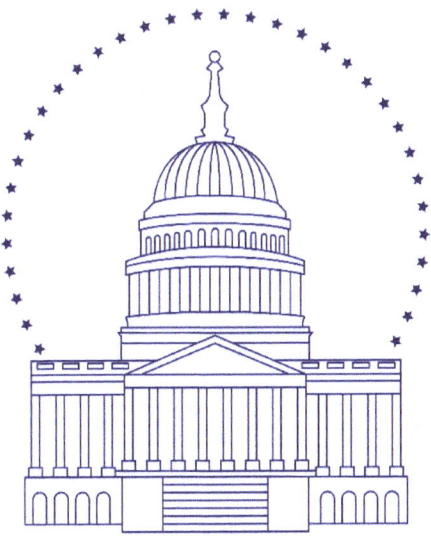

As I talk to people about moral issues and how to deal with the horrendous moral decline in modern society, it is not unusual at all to bump up against a particular dilemma. On the one hand, the majority of people don't seem to like the moral direction of our nation. On the other hand, they don't like the possibilities that exist for confronting it.

If an individual decides to put a focus on the spiritual side of things, it means that person must become bold in

Chapter 10

expressing his or her faith. That can be somewhat distressing for those who don't feel comfortable engaging others that way. The other possible focus is on cleaning up society using political means. This is also distressing for many because it requires getting down in the gutter of political compromise, where so much moral slime resides.

Obviously, there are those who are naturally bold about expressing their faith, and others who don't mind getting down and dirty in the gutter of politics. But the majority of Christians are not comfortable with either of these extremes. They would prefer to land somewhere in the middle. But even there, a certain amount of activism eventually becomes necessary.

The truth is, as Christians, we are called on to confront the culture with the claims of the gospel. And no matter what form that takes, we must be prepared to do it. In the Bible, we are admonished to be ready to express our faith. But there are times when doing that requires us to become active in some other way.

What we want to do here is to focus on the way Christians ought to think about engaging the political arena. As stewards of the gospel, we can't just ignore that part of life, especially in a democracy like ours – in spite of the ugliness that is often found there. So just how should we think about political activism?

www.ingramcontent.com/pod-product-compliance
Lightning Source LLC
Chambersburg PA
CBHW070116080526
44586CB00013B/1315

KILLING THE MYTH

Do You Believe in Separation of Church and State?

"Separation of church and state" has to be one of the most misunderstood concepts in America. Contrary to popular belief, it is not in the U.S. Constitution. In fact, it is not in America's legal code at all. Rather, it is a completely foreign notion that has entered the pop culture and, somehow, taken on a life of its own.

The term itself was an adaptation from a letter written by Thomas Jefferson to a group of Baptists in Connecticut. Jefferson was simply reassuring this group that he agreed with their contention that the federal government should not establish a state church nor impose a religious mandate on American citizens. Nowhere was there the notion that Christians, or anyone else for that matter, should be prohibited from expressing their personal faith in the public square.

Yet that is what this argument has come to be about. There are those who truly believe that there is a "neutral" point of view as it relates to values. Additionally, these same people typically contrast these "neutral" values with "religious" (particularly Christian) values.

In this book, Freddy Davis engages the notion of values as they are expressed in public life. His treatment of this topic begins by looking at where values really come from. He then answers key questions regarding the true nature of religious values and how the notion of separation of church and state should be addressed.

The Goal of Political Activism

In order to understand the nature of political activism, it is first necessary to grasp the goal of politics itself. It is impossible to be effective doing something that one doesn't fully grasp. To be honest, there are a lot of people who actually do try to engage the political process before they understand the nature of the system they want to influence. And, without exception, people who try to do that tend to get beat up pretty badly. I don't know how many people I have talked to who tell me they wish they had known more about the political system before they tried to influence it.

While politics generally has a negative reputation among the population at large, the purpose of politics is actually rather important. In fact, without a competent and efficiently operating political system, society would very quickly degenerate into chaos. The purpose of politics is to administer governmental entities. As such, it is not the existence or the goal of politics that is the problem. Rather, it is the process of "doing" politics that generates all of the unpleasantness.

In order for a society to operate smoothly, there must be a stable and working governmental system that provides a mechanism to maintain order in society. In every society, there are many actors who have competing agendas that they want to promote. Without a stable bureaucratic system to provide a means for this to be sorted out, people would have to simply use raw power and violence to get their way. So, instead of violence and raw power, we have a working political system where people can fuss, argue, and, yes, sometimes even resort to manipulation, in order to come up with solutions. But you must also realize that the kind of give and take necessary to make a governmental system operate can be extremely messy. And it is that messiness that turns people off.

So, political activism becomes a part of that messy system. People who wish to influence the direction of the government will find it necessary to, at some level, get down into the gutter and confront the people who oppose their position. Political activism is about engaging the political system in an effort to influence what is going on in society.

Different Worldview Perspectives on Political Activism

Various people have different perspectives on political activism. Some just love the rough and tumble of that environment and engage it, seemingly, just for sport. But most who become politically active have a different motivation. They want to influence the political system on behalf of some issue, or issues, they are passionate about.

But it is not just the fact of activism that is important as we consider this topic. The beliefs a person has about "how" to engage the process is, perhaps, even more important. As it turns out, people who hold different worldview perspectives actually engage the process differently.

We must understand, though, that this is not an issue related to an individual's sincerity. People of every persuasion will generally be quite sincere in their desire to impact the system for their cause. Rather, it has more to do with what is "right," and what kind of tactics are acceptable.

In American culture, of the various possibilities, there are mainly two opposing worldviews that tend to dominate the scene. The two are Naturalism and Christian Theism. Let's take a look at how people who follow these particular worldview systems tend to view the task of political activism.

Naturalism

Naturalism is the belief that the material universe, operating by natural laws, is all that exists. It does not believe in any kind of transcendent reality. As such, Naturalists assert that there is no God, so there can be no transcendent moral standard. For them, there is no alternative but that all morality must be derived from human opinion.

At this point the question becomes, "Which human beings get to set the moral standards?" And the bottom-line answer must be, "Those who have the power to enforce their will." Thus, Naturalism is based on the premise that there is no innately right or wrong belief or action. What is right and wrong can be whatever is acceptable to the people who must live by the standards that are set.

This also applies to the methods people use to advocate for their favorite cause. Of course, there are limits on what is acceptable within any given society. But the limits are not based on any kind of objective notion of right or wrong. It is based purely on what is acceptable in society.

As such, things that were once considered "wrong" to prior generations may become "right" for later ones. And methods of advocating for one's favorite cause are only limited by what is acceptable in the current social and political environment. This is also changeable over time.

Christian Theism

Christian Theism has an entirely different perspective. Based on biblical teachings, God exists, and He created the material universe and humankind for a purpose., In addition to that, He has revealed His purpose to humanity. And the way we act in relation to the political system fits into that purpose.

Based on Christian beliefs, the purpose of a political system is to create a stable environment that allows for God's work to be done on earth. It is not the work of government to focus on doing Christian ministry. That is the work of the church. But this does not mean that government is divorced altogether from God's will. Government ought to operate based on principles that are consistent with the values God has revealed to be right. When it does this, an environment is created in society that allows believers (the church) to do the work of God without hindrance. (Interestingly, it is this kind of environment that also makes it possible for people with other beliefs to freely advocate for their convictions, as well.)

Political Activism in America Vs. Other Places

Political activism will have very different expressions depending on the circumstances of the political system. For instance, places where power is concentrated in the hands of government officials – dictatorship, monarchy, oligarchy, communism/socialism – will not typically allow political dissent to be freely expressed. (It should be noted that these approaches to governing are normal expressions of a naturalistic worldview). In places where there is significant government control, the leaders typically suppress the citizens' ability to be active in ways that threaten those in power. Places where power is concentrated in the hands of the citizenry, however, generally do provide the opportunity for the citizens to be active in ways that could possibly threaten those who hold political power.

America is in the latter category. As a democratic republic, ultimate political power rests in the hands of the citizenry who elect people to represent their interests in the government. When the citizens don't like what is going on, they not only have the ability to vote their representatives out of office, they can also protest against government actions, and petition their representatives in order to redress grievances.

Chapter 10

Political Activity as Viewed by Christians and Non-Christians

But the fact that Americans have the right to be politically active does not address the entire scope of possibilities. There are different ways that political activity can be conducted – and the worldview beliefs of an individual will greatly influence what particular issues are promoted, as well as how political activism is carried out. Let's see how this plays out by comparing the approach of Naturalism to that of Christian Theism.

As was mentioned before, Naturalism is the belief that there is no supernatural existence. All that exists is the natural universe operating by natural laws. Since there is no God, there is no transcendent person in existence to reveal to mankind any objective moral standard. As such, it is up to human beings themselves to develop their own morality.

In doing this, the only possibility for creating a moral standard is for those with enough power and authority in society to decide the way they think things ought to be, then impose it on society. This is the approach Saul Alinsky pioneered as he developed his "Rules for Radicals" – a naturalistic methodology designed to teach people how to impose their desires on the populace.

His methodology involves the use of raw power to get one's way. People who live by a naturalistic worldview do not see anything morally wrong with doing whatever they need to do to get their way. For them, getting their way is the ultimate goal of political activism. For Naturalists, it is permissible to lie, cheat, steal, or use any other tactic, as long as they can get away with it.

Christian Theism, on the other hand, believes in God, and teaches that He has revealed what is morally right. It is, then, incumbent on Christians to understand that morality and live by it. Rather than a goal of getting one's own way, the goal of political activism for a Christian is to accomplish God's purposes.

This different mindset is expressed using an entirely different paradigm. Rather than seeking personal power, Christians recognize that the power is God's. They believe that He has placed human beings in the world as His agents who are to be stewards of His power in order to accomplish His purposes. As such, the means, as well as the ends, must be promoted in a way that corresponds to God's will.

When engaging political institutions based on a Christian worldview perspective, it is also important to understand that the purpose of those secular institutions is not to *directly* accomplish the spiritual purposes of God. That is the role of the church. Rather, government policy is to be God's instrument for creating an environment that allows His work to be done.

Individual Christians, then, should become personally involved in the political system based on God's particular calling in their life. Some should actually enter a profession that is connected to the political system. Others should be advocates before those in the political system for causes

Chapter 10

God has revealed to be a part of His will. And everyone should be an active voter to hold their representatives accountable. This is the work of a faithful steward of God given to Americans under our system of government.

To What Degree Should Christians Be Politically Active?

So, should Christians become politically active? Some would say, "No." The primary argument I hear in this regard is that politics is so dirty that Christians should just stay away from it. But if we took that attitude about all of life, we would not engage the sinful world at all.

It is not just politics that is full of dirtiness. The same can be said of business, media, education, entertainment, and even many charitable efforts to help the down and out in society. In fact, the list of places where evil resides in the world is practically endless.

The fact is, Jesus stepped out of paradise to live in the gutter of this sinful world for the very purpose of helping human beings get out of the gutter. He did not sacrifice His purity to do it, but He did have to get his hands dirty by reaching out and touching our dirtiness. Are we better than Jesus? No, we are not.

God calls believers out of the gutter of sin. At the same time, He does not do it in a way that allows us to escape helping those who still live in it. In fact, just the opposite. We, like Jesus, must be willing to get our hands dirty (though not our hearts).

So when it comes to politics, we must fulfill the responsibility God has placed on us. We must remember, God ordained government. And He ordained it to fulfill a specific purpose – to provide order in society so that His work could be accomplished.

It is very difficult to do God's work (or any work at all, for that matter) in an environment where there is chaos. And if God ordained government, He calls people to be involved in it who understand His ways and who have a heart for His purposes.

Actually, it is when people who don't know God get in power, that proper order begins to break down.

Certainly, the responsibility for interacting with government is not the same for everyone. There are various callings God places on people according to His purposes. I believe the calling to get involved in the political process can be broken down into three distinct categories.

First, there are those God has called to serve professionally in the political arena. Some of these are elected officials, but others would include those who serve in other parts of the governmental system. These are the people who create, implement, and adjudicate laws and policy so as to create an orderly society. God wants people who will govern by principles that correspond to His will to be in positions of power and authority, and He calls some to serve in that way.

Chapter 10

A second category relates to those who are involved in political advocacy outside of the structure of government. These are people who advocate for issues that are biblically based. Some of these people will work in organizations that do this professionally.

There are many Christian organizations that are engaged in political advocacy. But there are also many who do that in a more informal manner. This could be people who write their representatives, speak out in the public square on behalf of a godly cause, or even who sign petitions.

The third category actually involves every Christian. The American system of government, is a democratic republic. What that means is, the citizens elect people to represent them in the halls of government. In our form of government, the citizens are ultimately the ones responsible for the running of government.

Since government is ordained by God and we have been given this kind of oversight responsibility, that makes us responsible before God as stewards of the political process. As such, Christians have a responsibility to know the issues, follow the work of those who represent them, and hold their representatives accountable by letting them know how they should be carrying out their responsibilities based on God's guidance. We are especially responsible for voting – as that is the ultimate expression of stewardship for a Christian citizen under our American form of government.

Each person must discern from God the degree of direct participation they should have in the political process. That said, every believer must, at the very least, be informed and vote. That is the minimum obligation of a Christian based on the stewardship responsibility God has given us.